A

Literature Unit

for

Madeline

by Ludwig Bemelmans

Written by Cynthia Holzschuher

Teacher Created Materials, Inc.
P.O. Box 1040
Huntington Beach, CA 92647
©*1995 Teacher Created Materials, Inc.*
Made in U.S.A.

ISBN 1-55734-538-4

Illustrated by
Kathy Bruce

Cover Art by
Agi Palinay

Table of Contents

Introduction and Sample Lessons

Madeline has been one of the most popular characters in children's literature since her first book was published in 1939. She is small, mischievous, and full of energy. The stories have endured through the years because of rhyming texts, whimsical illustrations, and predictable situations that magically appeal to children who have never been to Paris or thought of attending a private parochial school. The six books in this series are wonderful classics that will provide a valuable look at French culture for your students. This unit is primarily concerned with the original title, *Madeline;* however, we hope you will also choose to share the other titles with your class. The appendix will help you with additional ideas. Many of the worksheets and activities in this unit are appropriate for any (or all) of the series.

A Sample Lesson Plan

The sample lessons on page 4 provide you with a specific set of lesson plan suggestions. Each of the lessons can take from one to several days to complete and can include all or some of the suggested activities. Refer to the "Suggestions for Using the Unit Activities" on pages 7–10 for information relating to unit activities.

A Unit Planner

If you wish to tailor the suggestions on pages 7–10 in a format other than that prescribed in the Sample Lesson Plan, a blank unit planner is provided on page 5. On a specific day you may choose the activities you wish to include by writing the activity number or a brief notation about the lesson in the "Unit Activities" section. Space has been provided for reminders, comments, and other pertinent information relating to each day's activities. Reproduce copies of the Unit Planner as needed.

Sample Lesson Plan

Lesson 1
- Read page 6 with the students to learn interesting facts about the author and the Madeline books.
- Locate Paris, France, on a world map.
- Read the story for enjoyment.
- Complete the story map. (page 19)
- Complete the Madeline character web. (page 18)

Lesson 2
- Introduce the vocabulary. (page 8)
- Reread the story, listening for the vocabulary words.
- Match the pocket chart riddles. (page 8)
- Discuss hospital (appendectomy) experiences. (page 9)
- Complete the "Dressing Madeline" activity. (page 36)
- Discuss the illustrations.

Lesson 3
- Brainstorm and sequence a list of events from the story.
- Complete the worksheet on Paris landmarks. (page 31)
- Reread the information about French children's school day. (page 32)
- Use the shape book pattern for the creative writing assignments or story questions. (page 41)
- Use the math manipulatives for graphing, patterning, and sorting activities. Play the card game. (page 26)
- Complete the rhyming word worksheet. (page 22)

Lesson 4
- Reread the story and encourage students to recite the opening lines.
- Make a Madeline doll. (page 38)
- Practice counting from 1–10 in French. (page 33)
- Practice telling time to the half hour. (page 30)
- Complete the antonym worksheet. (page 20)
- Make the Madeline pictionary. (page 25)

Lesson 5
- Complete the Madeline puzzle. (page 42)
- Work in groups to make stick puppet theaters and stick puppets. (pages 15–17)
- Practice the Readers' Theater. (page 44)
- Prepare the French luncheon (page 46) and watch a video.

Unit Planner

Unit Activities

Date:

Notes/Comments:

Unit Activities

Date:

Notes/Comments:

Unit Activities

Date:

Notes/Comments:

Unit Activities

Date:

Notes/Comments:

Unit Activities

Date:

Notes/Comments:

Unit Activities

Date:

Notes/Comments:

Getting to Know . . .

. . . the Author and the Madeline books

(Madeline is published in the U.S. and Canada by Scholastic Book Services, in U.K. by ScholasticPublishing Limited, and in Australia by Ashton Scholastic Party Limited.)

Ludwig Bemelmans was born April 27, 1898, in Meran, Tirol, Austria. His father was a painter and his mother, the daughter of a wealthy brewery owner. He attended public and private schools and immigrated to the United States at 16.

Bemelmans worked in a variety of hotel and restaurant jobs about which he later wrote. He studied art with a German artist, Thaddeus, in New York and eventually became a successful artist. Never really comfortable with exhibiting and selling his paintings, he began illustrating and writing books for a living. His books have won several awards; *Madeline* was the runner-up for the Caldecott Medal in 1940, and in 1953, the sequel, *Madeline's Rescue*, won the Caldecott.

Bemelmans became a naturalized citizen in 1918 and served as a German translator in the United States Army during World War I. In 1935 he married Madeline Freund, and together they had a daughter named Barbara. Ludwig died in 1962 and is buried in Arlington, Virginia.

Here are some interesting connections between events in Ludwig Bemelman's life and the events in his books.

- Ludwig Bemelmans' mother attended a convent school with straight rows of beds and wash basins like those illustrated in *Madeline*.

- Bemelmans himself attended a private school and remembered being the smallest boy in the class (like Madeline) and walking through town in straight lines with his classmates and teacher.

- Bemelmans was once hospitalized across from a girl who showed him her appendectomy scar. In that same hospital room there was a ceiling crack "that had the habit of sometimes looking like a rabbit." There was also a bed with a crank and a nurse carrying a tray.

- He once gave two neighbor girls 50 cents each because they originated the idea for the sequel, *Madeline's Rescue*. They suggested that a dog should go to the school, be sent away, and return to have enough puppies for each girl to have one.

- He actually observed the dog in *Madeline's Rescue* swimming the Seine River to retrieve an artificial leg. At the same time, a long line of little girls with their teacher was crossing the bridge above him.

Suggestions for Using the Unit Activities

Use some or all of the following suggestions to introduce students to Madeline and to extend their appreciation of the book through activities that cross the curriculum. The suggested activities have been divided into three sections to assist the teacher in planning the literature unit.

The sections are:

- **Before the Book:** suggestions for preparing the classroom environment and the students for the literature to be read

- **Into the Book:** activities that focus on the book's content, characters, theme, etc.

- **After the Book:** extends the reader's enjoyment of the book

Before the Book

1. Before you begin the unit, prepare the vocabulary cards, story questions, and sentence strips for the pocket chart activities. (See samples, patterns, and directions on pages 11–13.)

2. Explain to the students that there are six Madeline books. (Display the books in the series.) The one you will be reading first, *Madeline,* was a runner up for the Caldecott Medal in 1940, so you should take particular interest in the drawings.

3. Read about the author (page 6) to learn more about Ludwig Bemelmans. Be sure to point out that Mr. Bemelmans' wife was named Madeline and that he actually was the smallest boy in his private school class.

4. Build background and set the stage by asking the following questions and discussing the students' responses.

   - Who knows what a private boarding school is? Would you like to attend this type of school? Why or why not?

   - Who can find Paris, France, on the map? Use the encyclopedia to find out more about French culture, art, food, etc.

   - Have you ever been to the hospital as a patient or visitor? How did it feel?

5. Create a bulletin board display of all the information found about Paris, France, from the previous activity. You may also wish to use the information on Paris landmarks on page 31.

6. Display the cover of *Madeline.* Have the children look for any clues that might convey the story setting.

7. Discuss with the students what they could do if they had a friend who was in the hospital.

Into the Book

1. Pocket Chart Activities: Story Questions

Develop critical thinking skills with the story questions on page 14. The questions are based on Bloom's Taxonomy and are provided in each of Bloom's Levels of Learning. Reproduce several copies of the house pattern on page 13 and write a story question on each house. (See directions on page 11.)

Suggestions for Using the Unit Activities *(cont.)*

2. Pocket Chart Activities: Vocabulary Cards

Discuss the meanings of the following words in context before reading the different Madeline books in which they are introduced. Make several copies of the hat on page 13. Write the words below on the hats. Display the hats in a pocket chart. (See page 11 for directions to make a pocket chart.)

Madeline	Madeline and the Bad Hat	Madeline's Rescue
disaster	habitat	camomile
solemn	horrid	annual
appendix	vegetarian	inspection
crank	ambassador	trustee
tiptoeing	menagerie	disgrace
dialed	guillotine	embrace
	barbarian	vengeance

Madeline and the Gypsies	Madeline in London	Madeline's Christmas
gust	embassy	merchant
caravan	dobbins	francs
potent	crumpets	nutritious
crystal	encore	trance
leathery	mascot	profound
pelt	balcony	
voyage	sentry	

3. Pocket Chart Activities: Riddles, Sentences, Quotations

- Write riddles for the main characters: Madeline, Miss Clavel, and Dr. Cohn. Display them with pictures for a matching game in the pocket chart.
- Brainstorm a list of sentences retelling the important events from the story; display them in the pocket chart.
- Have students sequence the sentences in the order in which the events happened in the story.
- Use the sentences to retell the story.
- Divide the class into small groups and distribute a few sentence strips to each group. Ask the groups to act out the part of the story to which the sentences refer.
- Print some quotations on sentence strips. Print the name of the speaker on a separate card. Use them for a matching activity in the pocket chart.

Suggestions for Using the Unit
Activities *(cont.)*

4. Hospital Experiences

Discuss hospital experiences with the students. Has anyone actually had an appendectomy? Who has a scar? How do you think Madeline felt when she was alone at the hospital? Ask students whether there is someone in one of their families who works at a hospital. Maybe they could speak to the class.

5. Dressing for the Weather

Discuss the different types of clothing you may wear for different types of weather. Have students complete page 36 by drawing clothes on Madeline for a particlular type of weather they have chosen. Have students write stories to accompany their selections of clothes for Madeline.

6. Paris Landmarks

Look again at the illustrations in the book. Share other books or travel brochures showing landmarks in Paris. How does Paris look different from where you live? If you should be fortunate enough to know a French national, invite him/her to visit your class to talk about the country. Reproduce page 31 and discuss the different Paris landmarks. Discuss with students what they would find in each of the landmarks and why they are so important.

7. French School

Read the information about French children's school day on page 32. Discuss with the students orally the questions at the bottom of the page. Have students work in small groups to write what a perfect school day would be like for them.

8. Character Web

Madeline is the heroine of the stories. What are her characteristics? She is small, brave, active, a good friend, etc. Reproduce page 18 and have students complete character webs with information about her.

9. What's the Story?

Have students use the story map on page 19 to determine the setting, characters, problem, and solution elements in *Madeline*. If students are not familiar with this format, model the process with them, using the example on this page or one of your own choosing.

10. Creative Writing

Using the pattern on page 41, make a house stencil a little larger than the size of notebook paper. Trace and cut out the pattern on pieces of red construction paper. Use the creative writing suggestions on page 24. Have students select questions to write about. After students have finished, attach their completed writings to the centers of the houses. Display the houses on a wall or assemble into a Madeline Class book.

11. Math Games

Make the math manipulatives on pages 62 and 27. Use the manipulitives to play the card games suggested on page 26.

12. Recitation

Reread the book and encourage your students to "recite" the opening with you. It is easy to learn, and similar lines are repeated in the other five MAdeline books.

13. Storytelling

Use the patterns on pages 38–40 to make Madeline and Pepito dolls. Have students use them to retell the story on a story map showing the settings: house, exterior, street scene, hospital room, bedroom (with 12 beds).

14. Counting in French

For experience with the French language, practice counting to ten (*Berlitz Jr. French Dictionary*, Aladdin Books, 1992). If you share the book *Madeline's Rescue*, you may want to play the number game "Where's Genevieve?" on page 33.

Suggestions for Using the Unit
Activities *(cont.)*

15. Telling Time

Plan activities to practice telling time to the half hour. Have students complete page 30 about telling time to the half hour. (The little girls left the house every morning at half past nine.)

16. Pictionary

Reproduce and cut out the cards on page 25. Put them in ABC order and staple into books. Have students use their books for class discussions about events in the Madeline books. Students may also act out a part having to do with one of their pictionary cards. Some of the pictures are from the other titles.

17. Story Wheel

Copy pictures of the characters on page 43, cut them out, color them, and glue them around the edge of a 9" (22.86 cm) paper plate. Using a fastener, attach a pointer made of cardboard to the center of the plate. Students sit in a circle and take turns spinning the pointer. They may respond with a description of the character or recall events involving that character.

After the Book
Culminating Activities

Celebrate the literature unit with a day of enjoyment for students, teachers, and parents. Have students present the Readers' Theater production of *Madeline,* complete with a play, poetry, music, and food. Send student-made invitations to other classes, teachers, and parents. Include the following preparations and activities:

1. Stick Puppet Theater/Puppet Patterns

Prepare stick puppet theaters, following the suggestions and directions on page 15. Allow the students to construct puppets by coloring and cutting out the puppets and gluing them to tongue depressors or craft sticks. Follow the suggestions for using stick puppets found at the bottom of page 15.

2. Sing French Songs

Enjoy singing some common French children's songs such as "Frere Jacques," "Au Clair de la Lune," or "Alouette." Contact your local library for copies of these songs and their lyrics.

3. Readers' Theater Script

Use the Readers' Theater script on pages 44 and 45 to involve the students in drama. Suggestions for implementing a readers' theater format and script are provided on page 44. Use the follow-up questions below to discuss Madeline's hospital visit.

- Why did Madeline go to the hospital?
- Do you think Madeline was a good patient in the hospital?
- How did Madeline's classmates show that they were good friends?

4. French Luncheon

Plan a French luncheon using the menu on page 46. You may wish to watch a Madeline video at this time.

Pocket Chart Activities

Prepare a pocket chart for storing and using the vocabulary cards, the story question cards, and the sentence strips.

How to Make a Pocket Chart

If a commercial pocket chart is unavailable, you can make a pocket chart if you have access to a laminator. Begin by laminating a 24"x 36" (60 cm x 90 cm) piece of colored tagboard. Run about 20" (50 cm) of additional plastic. To make nine pockets, cut the clear plastic into nine equal strips. Space the strips equally down the 36" (90 cm) length of the tagboard. Attach each strip with cellophane tape along the bottom and sides. This will hold sentence strips, word cards, etc., and can be displayed in a learning center or mounted on a chalk tray for use with a group. When your pocket chart is ready, use it to display sentence strips, vocabulary words, and question cards. A sample chart is provided below.

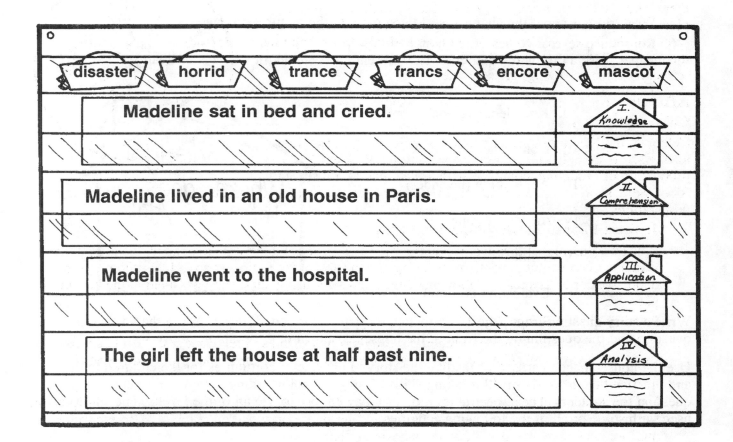

How to Use the Pocket Chart

1. On yellow construction or index paper, reproduce the hat-shaped pattern on page 13. Make vocabulary cards as directed on page 8. Print the definitions on sentence strips for a matching activity.

2. Select quotations from the stories and print them on sentence strips. Match the quotations to the speakers from the story.

Pocket Chart Activities (cont.)

3. Match the same quotations to the book titles in which they occur.

4. Print events from the story on sentence strips. Have students display them in sequential order.

"Little Madeline sat in bed, cried and cried — her eyes were red."

"'Good-bye,' they said, 'we'll come again,' and the little girls left in the rain."

5. Write riddles about the characters. Match them to the pictures on page 43.

6. Reproduce several copies of the house pattern (page 13) on six different colors of construction paper. Use a different paper color to represent each of Bloom's Levels of Learning.

    Example:

    I. Knowledge (green)

    II. Comprehension (pink)

    III. Application (lavender)

    IV. Analysis (orange)

    V. Synthesis (blue)

    VI. Evaluation (yellow)

Write a story question from page 14 on the appropriate color-coded house. Write the level of the question and the question on the front of the house, as shown in the example above.

Use the house-shaped cards after reading the story to provide opportunities for the children to develop and practice higher level critical thinking skills. Using the color coding system, you may choose to question the students at one specific level or you may choose to use all of the levels. The cards can be used with some or all of the following activities:

- Have a child choose a card, read it aloud, or give it to the teacher to read aloud. The child answers the question or calls on a volunteer to answer it.

- Pair children. The teacher reads a question. Partners take turns responding to the question.

- Play a game. Divide the class into teams. Ask for a response to a question written on one of the question cards. Teams score a point for each appropriate response. If question cards have been prepared for several different stories, mix up the cards and ask team members to respond by naming the story that relates to the question. Extra points can be awarded if a team member answers the question as well.

Pocket Chart Patterns

See pages 7 and 8 for directions.

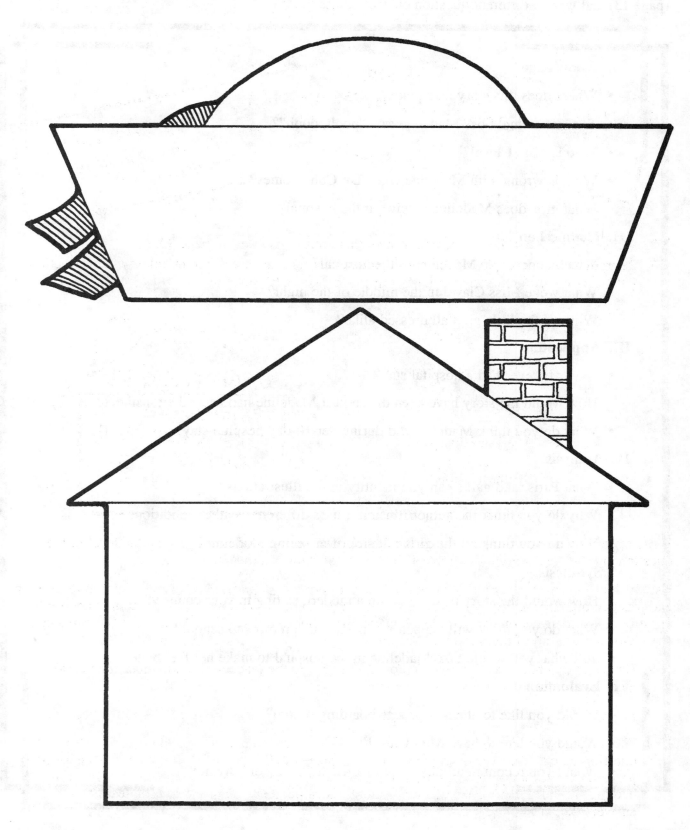

Story Questions

Use the following questions with the suggested activities on page 12. Prepare the house pattern (page 13) and write a different question on each house.

I. Knowledge

- Where does this story take place?
- To what animal does Madeline say, "pooh, pooh"?
- Who is Miss Clavel?
- What is wrong with Madeline when Dr. Cohn comes?
- What gifts does Madeline receive in the hospital?

II. Comprehension

- What happened to Madeline in the hospital?
- What woke Miss Clavel in the middle of the night?
- Why are the little girls all dressed alike?

III. Application

- Have you ever had a hospital stay?
- How would the story have been different if Madeline had needed a tonsillectomy?
- What do you think Madeline did during her 10-day hospital stay?

IV. Analysis

- What Paris landmarks can you identify in the illustrations?
- Why do you think the author/illustrator uses different weather conditions?
- Why do you think all the girls felt sick after seeing Madeline?

V. Synthesis

- How would the story be different in a modern setting in your country?
- What do you think will happen when Madeline returns to school?
- Tell what you would take Madeline in the hospital to make her feel better.

VI. Evaluation

- Would you like to attend a private boarding school?
- Would you like to have Miss Clavel's job?
- Would you recommend this book to a friend? Why or why not?

Stick Puppet Theaters

Make a class set of puppet theaters (one for each child), or make one theater for every two to four children.

Materials: 22" x 28" (56 cm x 71 cm) pieces of colored poster board (enough for each student or group of students); markers, crayons, or paints; scissors or craft knife

Directions:

1. Fold the poster board about 8" (20 cm) in from each of the shorter sides.
2. In the center of the theater, cut a "window" large enough to accommodate two or three puppets. (See illustration.)
3. Let the children personalize and decorate their own theaters.
4. Laminate the theaters to make them more durable. You may wish to send the theaters home at the end of the year or save them to use year after year.

Suggestions for Using the Puppets and Puppet Theaters:

- Prepare the stick puppets using the directions on page 16. Use the puppets and the puppet theaters with the Readers' Theater script on pages 44 and 45. (Let small groups of children take turns reading the parts and using the stick puppets.)
- Let children experiment with the puppets by telling the story in their own words.
- Read quotations from the book or make statements about the characters and ask students to hold up the stick puppets represented by the quotes or statements.

Stick Puppet Patterns

Directions: Reproduce the patterns on tagboard or construction paper. Color the patterns. Cut along the dotted lines. To complete the stick puppets, glue each pattern to a tongue depressor or craft stick. Use stick puppets with puppet theaters and/or the readers' theater script.

Stick Puppet Patterns *(cont.)*

See page 16 for directions.

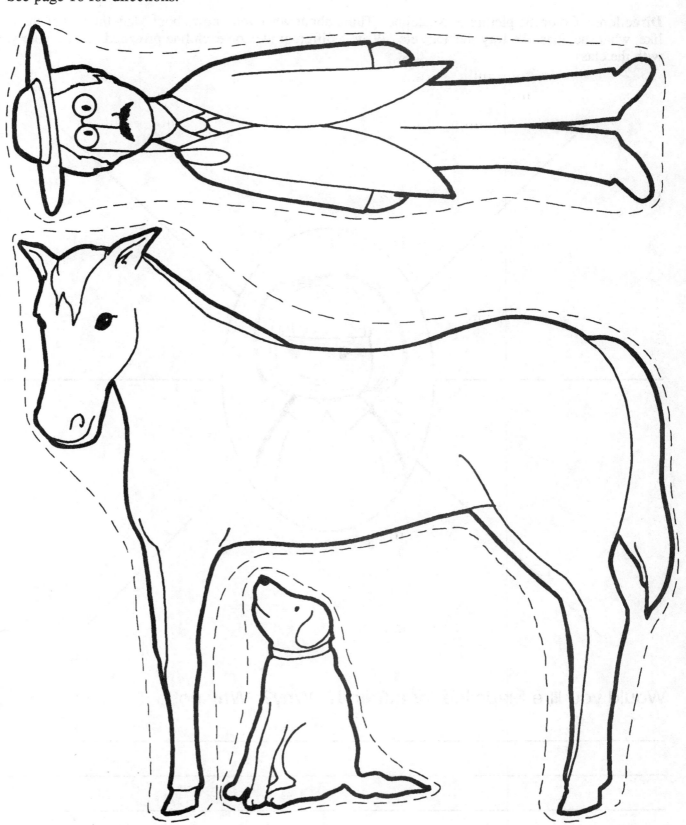

Name_____

Character Web

Directions: Color the picture of Madeline. Think about what you know about Madeline; what she is like, what she does, the way she acts, etc. Write a different idea on each line provided. Share your web with the class.

Would you like Madeline for a friend? Why? Why not?

_____

_____

_____

18

Name_____

What's the Story?

Use this story map to summarize the characters, setting, problem, and solution for the Madeline book of your choice.

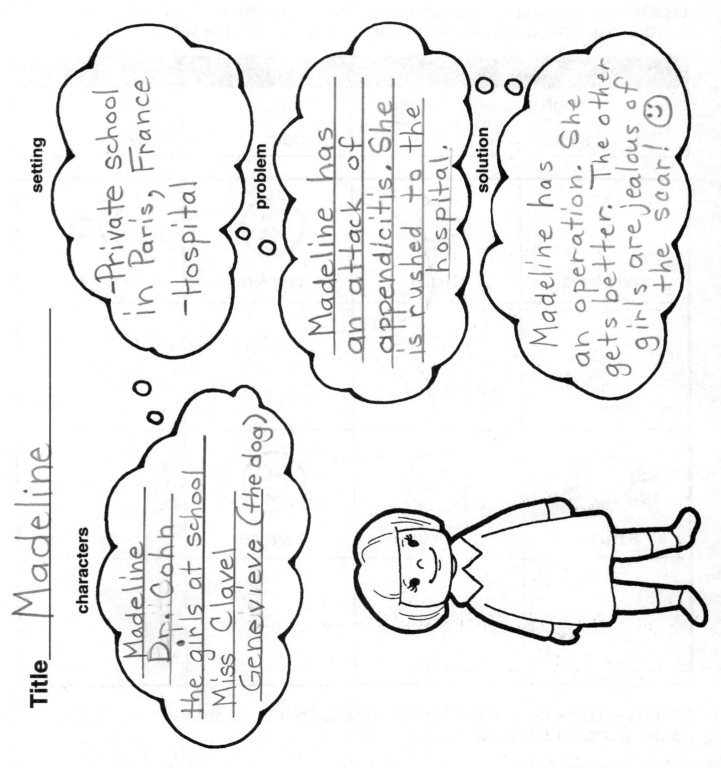

setting

-Private school in Paris, France
-Hospital

problem

Madeline has an attack of appendicitis. She is rushed to the hospital.

solution

Madeline has an operation. She gets better. The other girls are jealous of the scar! ☺

Title Madeline

characters

Madeline
Dr. Cohn
the girls at school
Miss Clavel
Genevieve (the dog)

Name_____

Antonyms

An antonym is a word that means the opposite of another word. Examples: hot—cold, soft—hard

Use the word bank to find words that are opposites. Print the opposite word in the space and draw a picture to show the meaning.

Word Bank			
laugh	asleep	day	large
smile	rain	dark	straight

crooked	**light**	**frown**	**night**
shine	**cry**	**awake**	**small**

*Bonus—Think of a way to draw pictures that illustrate these antonym pairs: good/bad and fast/slow.

Name _____

Following Directions

Madeline and the girls visited Pepito in London for his birthday.

Follow these directions to finish the picture.

- Color the cake icing pink.
- Add eight candles to the top of the cake.
- Print "Pepito" on the front of the cake.
- Draw a bow in each little girl's hair.
- Choose one color. Color all the girls' dresses the same.
- Color Pepito's suit blue. Draw a balloon in his hand.

Name_____

Rhyming Words

Directions: Cut a word from the bottom of the page that rhymes with one of the following words. Glue it to the right of the rhyming word.

light		bed	
sad		sky	
hat		cry	
mice		vines	
far		drank	

Rhyming Words

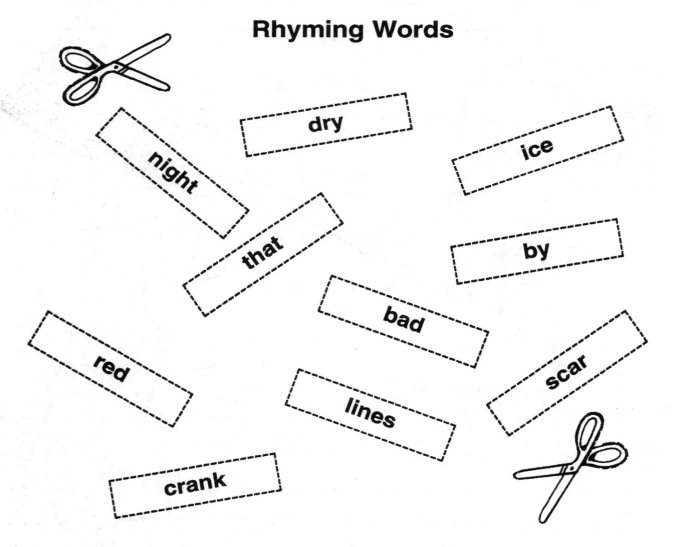

Name_____

A Magic Carpet Ride

Where would you go if you had a chance to ride a magic carpet? Draw a picture of yourself on the carpet and write a story to tell where you are going. Why did you choose that location?

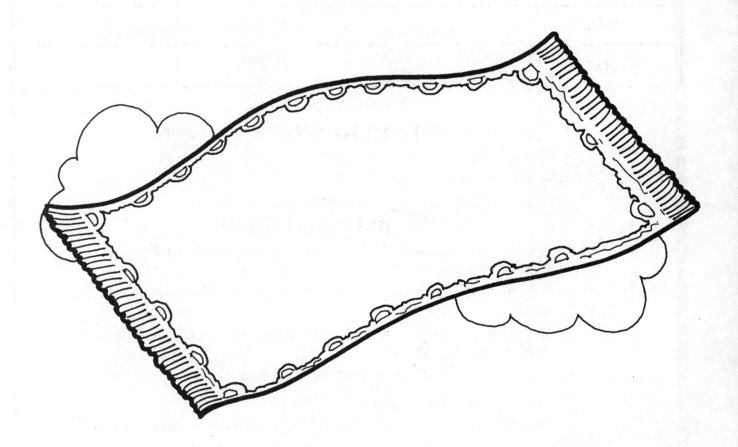

I am going to _____

because _____

_____

_____.

Creative Writing

See page 9, item number 10, for directions.

Madeline

- What kinds of things did Madeline do to frighten Miss Clavel?
- Have you ever visited someone in the hospital? Write about the experience.
- Would you like to go to a private boarding school? Why? Why not?

Madeline and the Bad Hat

- Do you know anyone who is a "Bad Hat"?
- What would happen if someone let all the zoo animals out of their cages?
- Would Pepito be a good friend? Why? Why not?
- Do you think Madeline liked Pepito?

Madeline's Rescue

- Do you have a dog? Can it do tricks? Did it ever have puppies?
- How would you feel if your dog ran away?
- What should you do if you fall into a river?
- What are safety rules that could have helped Madeline?

Madeline and the Gypsies

- Have you ever been to a carnival? Have you ever ridden a Ferris wheel? Write about the experience.
- Have you ever taken a trip by plane, ship, or train? What were your favorite parts of your trip?
- Do you think Madeline and Pepito were happy with the Gypsies? How could you tell?

Madeline in London

- Have you ever planted a garden? Write about the experience.
- What do you think the horse's life was like with the girls at the school?
- Have you ever had a friend who moved? Were you lonely?
- How did Pepito prepare for the arrival of the girls?

Madeline's Christmas

- What chores did Madeline do when she was sick?
- Write about the last time you were sick.
- Do you believe in magic?
- How would Christmas have been different without the magician?

Madeline Pictionary

Directions: Color the pictures. Cut apart the pages. Put them in ABC order and staple into a book. Use your book for class discussions about events in the Madeline books.

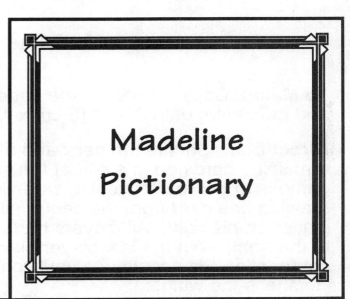

Madeline
Pictionary

Madeline

Pepito

Spanish
flag

tiger

Patterns and Card Game

Madeline Card Game
(for 3–4 players)

To Make: Copy six sets of the patterns on pages 26 and 27. Cut apart and glue them onto 3"x 5" (8 cm x 13 cm) cards.

Directions: Shuffle the deck and deal five cards to each player. The remaining cards go in a pile at the center of the table. The object of the game is to get four matching cards in your hand. The dealer begins by drawing one card from the center pile and trading away one card to the player on his right. All players trade off cards around the table, (in order; to the right), with the last player placing one card at the bottom of the center pile. Play continues until someone has four matching cards. He/she is the winner.

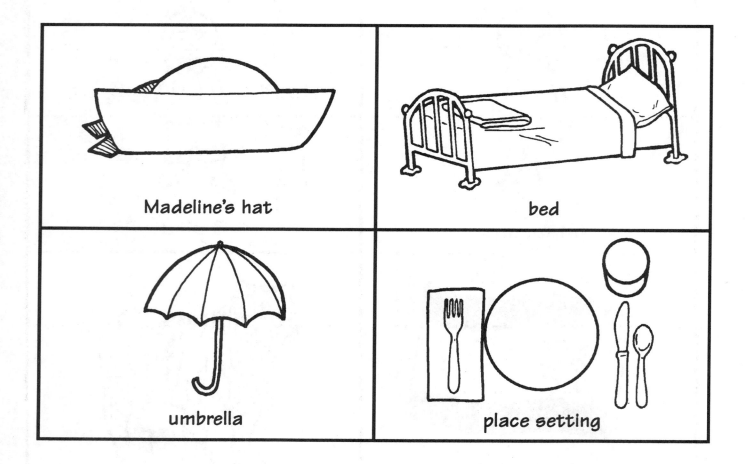

Madeline's hat

bed

umbrella

place setting

Note: You may also use the cards in pairs for a concentration-style matching game.

Patterns and Card Game (cont.)

toothbrush

carpet

dog

French flag - blue, white, red

Eiffel Tower

horse

house

lion

Name _____

Word Problems

To the teacher: These problems are designed so that you can make them appropriate to a number of different skill levels. Fill in the blanks with numbers of your choosing.

Money

1. If a student pass to the zoo costs _____ ¢, how much will it cost for twelve girls to go to the zoo? _____ Compare this cost to the admission price at the zoo where you live.

2. If student bus fare is _____ ¢, how much did it cost the girls to go to visit Madeline? (Remember, there are only 11). Add Miss Clavel's fare of _____. What is the total cost? _____ Compare the cost to the bus fare where you live.

3. *Madeline's Christmas*—If one rug cost _____ francs, how much did Madeline pay for 12 rugs? _____

Time

1. If the girls left school at "half past nine" (9:30), and it took _____ minutes to walk to the zoo, what time would it be when they arrived?

2. Madeline's appendectomy took two hours. If she got to the hospital at _____:00, what time did she awaken? _____

3. *Madeline in London*—If the plane arrived in London at "half past nine" (9:30), and the trip took half an hour, when did the plane leave Paris? _____

Calendar Skills

1. Madeline was in the hospital ten days before Miss Clavel and the girls went to visit. If she went to the hospital on _____ (date), on what date did she have visitors? _____

2. *Madeline's Rescue*—Genevieve was at the school for six months before the inspection on May 1. About what date do you think she rescued Madeline from the Seine River? _____

3. *Madeline and the Bad Hat*—The story mentions all four seasons: spring, summer, autumn, and winter. Look for other phrases that mark the passage of time ("year in year out"). Try to estimate the amount of time covered by this story. _____

Name_____

Classify and Graph Pictures

Directions: After reading the book, *Madeline and the Gypsies*, look through the book again and count the number of pictures and make a graph.

_____ Madeline in circus costume   _____ Pepito in circus costume

_____ Madeline in school dress   _____ Pepito in suit

Madeline and Pepito Pictures

Each square stands for one drawing.

Name_____

Telling Time to the Half Hour

In each story, Madeline and her friends "left the house at half past nine." That means they left at 9:30. Look at the clock to understand 30 minutes past the hour. Add hands to the clocks and write the times on the clocks below.

time to wake up
half past seven

time to eat breakfast
half past eight

time to go walking
half past nine

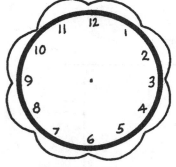

time for lunch
half past twelve

time to play with Genevieve
half past two

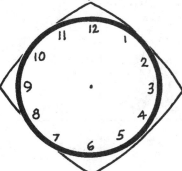

time to visit Pepito
half past three

time for dinner
half past six

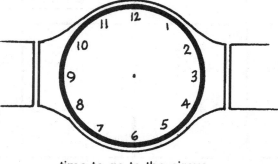

time to go to the circus
half past seven

time for bed
half past nine

Paris Landmarks

Madeline went to school in Paris, the capital city of France. The city has many beautiful buildings that attract tourists. Paris is also important as a center of art, culture, and fine food. Here are some of the landmarks illustrated in *Madeline*:

Eiffel Tower

This is the highest point in Paris and the symbol of the city. There are three observation floors with restaurants and souvenir shops. It attracts 3.5 million visitors a year.

Opera House

This is the largest opera theater in the world. The beautiful lobby is made of marble. There is also an opera museum inside. It took ten years (1862–1872) to build the hall and museum.

The Place Vendome

This public square got its name because it once was the residence of the Duke of Vendome. The buildings are simple but include the famous Hotel Ritz and the home where Chopin died.

Hotel Invalides

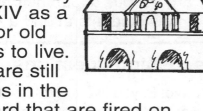

This hotel was built in 1671 by Louis XIV as a place for old soldiers to live. There are still cannons in the courtyard that are fired on important holidays.

Notre Dame

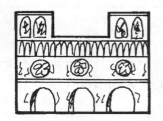

This is one of the finest cathedrals in the world. It has two towers and 28 stone statues of the kings of France over the doors. Inside is a museum with religious artifacts.

The Louvre

This art museum holds some of the most famous paintings and sculptures in the world. It was originally built as a fortress in the 13th century. It is near the Seine River.

French Children's School Day

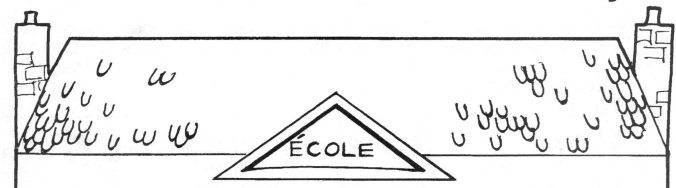

ÉCOLE

French children attend school four days a week from 8:00 a.m.–4:30 p.m. They also go to school for three hours on Saturday morning. There is no school on Wednesdays. In the elementary grades, children from ages 6–11 spend most of their day learning reading, writing, and arithmetic. Less time is spent on history, civics, art, music, and physical education. All textbooks and school supplies are provided free of charge by the government. There are no religious classes permitted in French public schools although it is a Roman Catholic country.

The lunch break is up to 2 hours long so children can go home for their big meal of the day. After eating, some children use the time at home for music practice or finishing homework. On Wednesdays, French children participate in organized sports like handball, soccer, and swimming. French students are serious about their education. The country has a 99% literacy rate, and many students attend a university.

Discussion questions

1. Would you like to go to school on the French schedule? (off Wednesday, longer days, attend on Saturday morning)

   _____

2. How would you use a two-hour lunch break?

   _____

3. Would you prefer to go home for lunch?

   _____

4. How is French school like/unlike the schools in your country?

   _____

5. How is French school today like/unlike Madeline's school?

   _____

Extension: Write a story about your ideal school day.

Where's Genevieve?

Skill: The students will read and say number words in French.

To Make: Make six copies of the patterns below. You will need 12 beds and one dog. Print a number word in French (and a digit from 0–11) on each bed. Color and cut out the pictures. Mount them on tagboard and laminate, if possible.

To Play: Arrange the beds in two lines of six in numerical order. Choose one child to hide the dog under a bed. The other players take turns guessing (in French) the location of the dog. The player who finds the dog may hide her for the next round.

French Numbers: zero, un, deux, trois, quatre, cinq, six, sept,
huit, neuf, dix, onze

Spain

Spain and Portugal together make up the Iberian Peninsula. They are to the south of France, separated by the Pyrenees Mountains. The capital city of Spain is Madrid, located almost in the center of the country. It is the largest city and has lovely parks, museums, shops, and cafes. Spain is a Roman Catholic country, and there are many religious holidays during the year when people take part in special festivities. Every large city has a plaza de toros (bull ring) where there are bull fights on fiesta (festival) days. The toreros (bullfighters) are highly trained and respected by the people. Attending bull fights is a traditional form of Spanish entertainment.

People in Spain get up early so that they can do most of their work before the heat of the day. They break at 2:00 p.m. for a two-or three-hour lunch and siesta (afternoon nap) and return later for about two more hours of work. The evening meal is at 10:00 p.m. and can last until midnight. Spanish food is highly seasoned, and a typical evening meal consists of vegetables, salad, meat or fish, and a dessert of fruit and cheese. Spanish families often share a home, so it is common for aunts, uncles, cousins, and grandparents to live and take their meals together. Children in Spain must attend school until the age of 14 when they take an examination to determine whether they will go to secondary school.

Short answer:

1. What is the capital of Spain? _____

2. What is the religion of Spain? _____

3. Where does a bull fight take place? _____

4. Who is a torero? _____

5. When does the siesta begin? _____

6. How long must Spanish children attend school? _____

Write a story telling what Pepito's life would be like if he lived in Spain.

34

London

Madeline and her father went to London to visit Pepito. It is the capital of England and has many beautiful and historic landmarks. London is important to the world as a center for tourism and trade and is the home of England's royal family. Here is some information about the locations pictured in *Madeline in London:*

Trafalgar Square
The site of St. Martin-in-the-Fields church and the National Gallery, this open square is marked with fountains and statues of lions. People gather here for political rallies and holiday celebrations.

Big Ben
The clock in Victoria Tower at Parliament Square first chimed the hour in 1859. It is named after its builder, Sir Benjamin Hall, and weighs about five tons.

Buckingham Palace
The home of Britain's royal family since Queen Victoria. Tourists enjoy watching the Changing of the Guard ceremony every day at noon.

The Tower of London
This medieval fortress houses the Crown Jewels, White Tower, Armories, Chapel of St. John, and several towers which held notable prisoners throughout history.

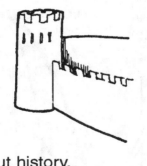

Tower Bridge
This drawbridge over the River Thames has two towers joined by a walkway. The roadway lifts so that large ships can pass by.

Whitehall
A street lined with large government buildings, it is the location of Churchill's Cabinet War Rooms, the Prime Minister's residence, and the Horse Guards' Parade.

Extension: Do research to learn about three additional London churches, museums, or landmarks. If possible, share tourist brochures and photographs.

Name_____

Dressing Madeline

Dress Madeline so that she is ready to go out in rain, snow, or sunshine. When finished coloring, write a story to go with your drawing.

Madeline in the

_____
                    (title)

It is _____.

Madeline is wearing her

_____.

She will _____

_____.

Next she will _____

_____

_____

_____

_____.

Then she will_____

_____

_____

_____

_____.

Name_____

Your Pet and Genevieve

Directions: Complete this chart with answers about your pet and Genevieve, the dog who saved Madeline. (If you do not have a pet, write about a pet you wish you had.)

Questions	Genevieve	Your pet—— *name*
Where did he/she come from?		
Where does he/she sleep?		
Can he/she do any tricks?		
What does he/she eat?		
How does he/she get exercise?		
What would you do if he/she was lost?		

Genevieve had twelve puppies, enough for each little girl to have one. What kinds of things would you need if you got a new puppy? Draw pictures of the things you would buy and label them with the words in the word bank.

Word Bank: bone, bed, leash, collar, food, water dish, toys

Madeline and Pepito Dolls

Madeline

You will need: a cardboard tube
yellow or blue and white scrap paper
patterns on page 39
glue stick
transparent tape
crayons
scissors
about 8" (20 cm) black yarn

Directions: You should decide if you want to dress Madeline in her yellow coat or her blue school dress. Choose the correct colored paper and cut out the pieces you will need from the patterns on page 39. Draw in Madeline's face and hair with your crayons. Color her shoes, gloves, tie, and buttons as you wish. Glue or tape pieces onto the cardboard tube. Allow them to dry thoroughly. Add the black yarn to her hat. Sit Madeline on the edge of your desk when you listen to her stories.

Pepito

You will need: a cardboard tube
blue, red, black and white scrap paper
patterns on page 40
glue stick
transparent tape
crayons
scissors

Directions: Pepito may wear a suit of red, blue, or black. His hat may match his suit or be black. Choose the colors you like and cut the pieces for Pepito from the patterns on page 40. Color his face, hair, shoes, and socks. Glue or tape the pieces onto the cardboard tube. Allow them to dry thoroughly. Sit Pepito on the edge of your desk when you read *Madeline and the Bad Hat, Madeline and the Gypsies,* and *Madeline in London.*

Madeline and Pepito Dolls *(cont.)*

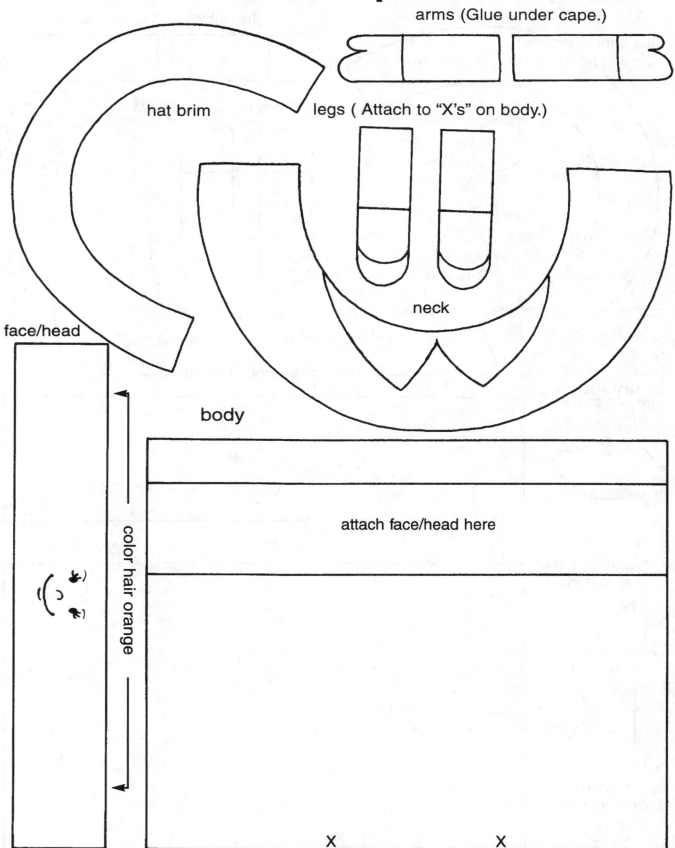

arms (Glue under cape.)

hat brim

legs (Attach to "X's" on body.)

neck

face/head

body

color hair orange

attach face/head here

X   X

Madeline and Pepito Dolls *(cont.)*

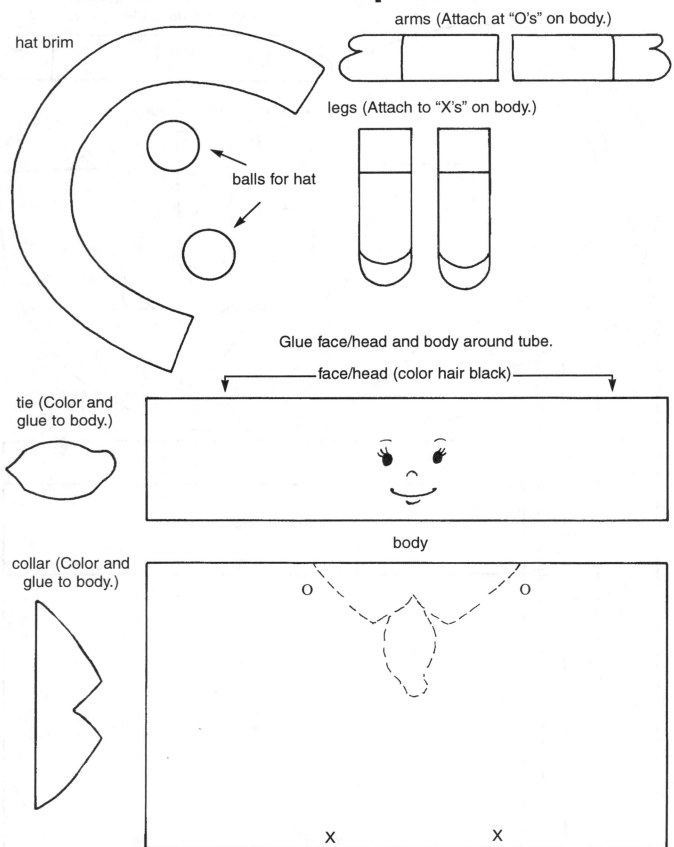

hat brim

arms (Attach at "O's" on body.)

balls for hat

legs (Attach to "X's" on body.)

Glue face/head and body around tube.

tie (Color and glue to body.)

face/head (color hair black)

body

collar (Color and glue to body.)

Shape Book Cover
House

Madeline Puzzle

Directions: Cut the pieces apart and glue them to another piece of paper. Color the picture. What was Madeline showing her friends?

Madeline Clip Art

See page 10, item 17, for directions.

Miss Clavel

Genevieve

Pepito

Madeline

Genevieve

Readers' Theater

Readers' theater provides an easy opportunity for students to perform a mini-play without the use of props, sets, costumes, or memorization. The dialog may be read as written or used as a basis for further elaboration.

Characters: Madeline   Jeanette
                               Miss Clavel   Claudia
                               Dr. Cohn   Narrator

The Hospital Visit

Miss Clavel - We must finish our lessons early today, girls. We are going to the hospital to visit Madeline.

Jeannette - Oh, Miss Clavel, may we?

Claudia - Oh yes, Miss Clavel, we've missed Madeline so. May we take her some toys and some candy?

Miss Clavel - Come now, girls. Put away your books. Get your coats and hats. Bring the gifts. I have some school work for Miss Madeline.

Narrator - They walked to the corner and waited at the bus stop. The bus trip was short and uneventful. Everyone was quiet. They were wondering how Madeline would be feeling. When she left the old house she was very sick. They had never seen Madeline cry. On the walk to the hospital gate, the girls passed a flower market.

Jeannette - Miss Clavel, may we take some flowers to Madeline?

Miss Clavel - Yes, I suppose that would be nice.

Narrator - They selected some flowers and entered the hospital. They made their way down the long hall to Madeline's room. They entered and found Madeline playing with a new doll house, a gift from her father.

Madeline - Welcome, my friends, please come in.

Jeanette - Look Madeline, we've brought you flowers…

Claudia - …and gifts. Here is some peppermint candy.

Readers' Theater *(cont.)*

Miss Clavel - Madeline, I brought you a book to read and your arithmetic book so that you can keep up with your lessons.

Madeline - Oh, thank you for all of these gifts. I will share them with the other children in the hospital, and Miss Clavel, I will try to do my arithmetic assignments. You know how difficult arithmetic is for me. It is not easy to be in the hospital for so long. I get bored. I am not really sick any more.

Narrator - While Madeline was talking with her friends, Dr. Cohn came in.

Dr. Cohn - Good afternoon, Madeline, how are you feeling?

Madeline - I'm feeling fine, Dr. Cohn. I'd like you to meet my friends from school. You've met my teacher, Miss Clavel.

Dr. Cohn - Yes, we've met. (*to the girls*) You know, Madeline was a sick little girl when she came to the hospital. A bad appendix can be very serious. (*to Madeline*) So Madeline, are you positive you're feeling well? No temperature? No pains?

Madeline - No. No...nothing. I'm feeling fine. When may I leave the hospital? I don't really like the food here...I'm tired of jello and chicken soup every day.

Dr. Cohn - Hmmm, is that right? (*He smiles.*) Very well, Madeline. I'll see what I can do. In the meantime, you rest. You've had an operation and no matter how well you think you feel, you need to stay quiet.

Narrator - Dr. Cohn left the room, and the girls continued to talk and look through Madeline's cards and gifts. In a short while Miss Clavel called them together.

Miss Clavel - Little girls, gather round Madeline's bedside. I will read you all a story before we leave.

Narrator - The girls gathered around, and Miss Clavel read *Rosebud* by Ludwig Bemelmans. Everyone was very calm, and when the story was finished they looked at Madeline and... she had fallen asleep! The girls got up quietly and tiptoed out of their friend's room. They felt happy as they made their way to the bus stop. They knew Madeline was doing well. They would return to the old house for dinner, and Madeline would be home soon.

French Luncheon and Videos

Set aside an afternoon for enjoying a French luncheon and several Madeline videos. If you wish, you may include the readers' theater (pages 44 and 45) and the singing of familar French folk songs.

These videos should be available at your library:

Madeline (Learning Corporations of America, 1952).

Madeline and the Bad Hat (Weston Woods, 1959).

Madeline's Rescue (Golden Book Video, 1988).

Madeline and the Gypsies (Golden Book Video, 1990).

Madeline in London (Golden Book Video, 1993).

Madeline's Christmas (Golden Book Video, 1991).

Luncheon Menu

Soup du jour - French onion soup

French bread

French croissants

Brie or Camembert cheese

Crackers

Assorted fruit platter

Apple cider

Recipe for French Onion Soup

(for six)

2 large onions, sliced

¼ cup (60 mL) margarine

4 cups (about 2 liters) of water

6 beef bouillon cubes

In a Dutch oven, cook the onions in the margarine until they are soft. Add water and bouillon cubes. Simmer, covered 15-20 minutes.

Bibliography

Other books by Ludwig Bemelmans:

Madeline (pop-up book). Viking, 1987.

Parsley. Harper, 1958.

Rosebud. Random House, 1942.

Sunshine. Simon and Schuster, 1950.

Related Fiction:

Henri's Walk to Paris by Leonore Klein. Addison Wesley, 1963.

A French School for Paul by Merelle Marovia. Lippincott, 1963.

Books by Francois Seignobosc, Scribner's Publishing

> *Jeanne-Marie at the Fair,* 1959.
>
> *Jeanne-Marie Counts Her Sheep,* 1951.
>
> *Jeanne-Marie in Gay Paris,* 1956.
>
> *Noel for Jeanne-Marie,* 1953.
>
> *Springtime for Jeanne-Marie,* 1955.
>
> *What Time Is It, Jeanne-Marie?,* 1963.

Related Nonfiction:

World Cities: London by James Davis and Sharryl Davis Hawkes. Raintree, 1990.

Inside Great Britain by Ian James. Watts, 1988.

Places and People of the World–Spain by Arthur Miller. Chelsea House, 1989.

A Family in France by Mary Regan. Lerner, 1988.

Let's Visit Spain by Ronald Seth. Burke Publ., Ltd., 1984.

We Live in France by James Tomlin. Bookwright Press, 1983.

Appendix

Here are some ideas to help you get started with the other Madeline titles.

Madeline's Rescue

- Brainstorm a list of names for the 12 puppies.
- Play "Where's Genevieve?" and practice French number words.
- Complete the activity on page 37 about pets.
- Write a sequel, explaining how the girls and Miss Clavel dealt with 12 puppies.
- Call the SPCA in your area to arrange a visit and a discussion about pet care and adopting stray animals.
- Make a list of places where dogs are not allowed (stores, restaurants, etc.).
- Discuss how the story would have been different had Madeline not fallen into the river. How else might they have gotten the dog?

Madeline and the Bad Hat

- Make a list of the bad things that Pepito did in the story.
- Would Pepito make a good friend? Why? Why not?
- Learn more about Spain (page 34).
- Brainstorm a list of foods for vegetarians.
- Complete the math word problems on page 28.
- Complete a character web for Pepito.
- Design yourself a "Bad Hat."

Madeline and the Gypsies

- Classify and graph the pictures on page 29.
- Share the experience of visiting a carnival or circus. Make a list of common attractions.
- Discuss how the characters Madeline, Pepito, and Miss Clavel felt during the story when they were lost and then found.
- Discuss/write: Would you like to be a circus performer? What would you choose to do? Why?

Madeline in London

- Read and discuss the London information on page 35. Look at travel brochures.
- Discuss/write: What happened on your last birthday?
- Research the career of a veterinarian. If possible, interview a veterinarian.
- Do you think Miss Clavel really wanted to keep the horse?
- Complete the Following Directions activity on page 21.
- Write a sequel, telling what happened to the horse in Paris.

Madeline's Christmas

- Discuss/write: How could you help your family if everyone were sick?
- Make a list of the chores Madeline did in the story.
- If possible, look at some French francs. How are they the same/different from our money?
- Share several books of simple magic tricks. Encourage students to read them and to try to perform the tricks.
- Complete the "Magic Carpet Ride" worksheet on page 23.

48